Enjoying Mass

Enjoying Mass

A resource for teachers and catechists

Joan Brown SND

kevin mayhew

First published in 2002 by
KEVIN MAYHEW LTD
Buxhall, Stowmarket, Suffolk IP14 3BW
Email: info@kevinmayhewltd.com

Scripture texts adapted from the New Jerusalem Bible.

9 8 7 6 5 4 3 2 1 0

ISBN 1 84003 973 6
Catalogue No 1500544

Cover design by Angela Selfe
Edited and typeset by Elisabeth Bates
Printed and bound in Great Britain

CONTENTS

INTRODUCTION

Enjoying Mass contains a wide range of activities and ways of celebrating which will enable children to use their gifts to minister in worship. This is to ensure that liturgy for children will not remain empty rituals, words and symbols but a way of life celebrated. This book will help children to celebrate Mass with understanding and responsibility and with a richer sense of participation and enjoyment.

In the first part of this book teachers and catechists are guided through the structure of the Mass, and the purpose of the many rites and elements which make up the liturgy of the Mass are explained. Notes on liturgical practice for celebrating the Mass with children are also included.

The second section of this book presents celebrations of liturgies based on the various elements of the Mass. Celebrations of prayers, penitential rite, liturgy of the word, etc., gradually build up into a celebration of the Mass. By being introduced to and learning to prepare and celebrate these individual elements, children become familiar with them. In this way children are led towards a deeper understanding of the Mass – the Eucharist – which is at the heart of all liturgical celebrations in the Catholic Community.

See also: *Catechism of the Catholic Church, 1187-1199.*
Directory of Children's Masses, 1973.
Liturgy of the Word with Children – Guidelines. Bishops' Conference of England and Wales, 1996.

SR JOAN BROWN, SND

LITURGY

- Public worship of the Church.
- A community action.
- Participation of the people of God in the work of God.
- Public worship of the people of God in union with Christ their High Priest.

Abba Father

- In liturgy we are caught up into the great love of Christ for the God he calls 'Father' and in the prayer he offers eternally to God.
- Deeply woven through the fabric of our lives, liturgy is what makes us a community.
- It is what forms and holds us together.

I believe

- It is the way in which we celebrate our faith.
- In liturgy the whole of our lives and even the tiniest details that make up our lives are gathered into God and blessed.
- Liturgy enables us to become more aware of God's great love and involvement in our lives and to celebrate it.

- Liturgy is always a community action in which God is praised and worshipped.

- It is the source from which the life of the community flows and the summit towards which all the activity of the community is directed.

- It is the right and the duty of all who are baptised.

- It builds up and strengthens the community.

- Liturgical celebrations involve signs and symbols: fire, water, oil, wine, bread, ash, etc., relating to the earth; washing, anointing, breaking bread, etc., related to human life on earth. It involves all the senses.

- Integral to liturgy is the Proclamation of the Word of God.

- Sacred music, silence, stillness and gesture can enrich the prayer and participation of the community.

- The use of sacred images can focus attention, heighten awareness and nourish faith.

- The Church's Calendar unfolds the whole mystery of Christ throughout the year. Celebrating the Feast Days and Festivals of the Church's year remind us of the coming of the Lord and of our union with the saints in heaven.

See also: *Catechism of the Catholic Church, 1187-1199.*
Liturgy of the Word with Children – Guidelines. Bishops' Conference of England and Wales, 1996.

Children are natural liturgists.
They see what we no longer see.
They sense what we have long forgotten.
Their imaginations know no boundaries.
They are full of awe and wonder.
They delight in mystery, ritual and symbol.
Liturgy is a child's world.

'Unless you become as little children you cannot enter the kingdom of Heaven.' Matthew 19:14

How can we adults enter a child's world? Only by enabling children to celebrate liturgy in a way appropriate and relevant to their age, experience and understanding, fostering a genuine sense of celebration. Then children will enjoy liturgy and want to be there. They will grow in faith, which grows when well-expressed in liturgy celebrated in such a way that its full meaning shines out clearly. They will be brought to Christ to be touched by him and with him stand in the Father's presence. This does not mean that everything in the liturgy will be fully understood by the children.

We can marvel at the wonders of creation, be uplifted by them, without understanding every detail of how they come about.

Giving children time and opportunities to celebrate enable them to become aware of what they value, what they give worth to in their lives, and how best to acknowledge and express this.

'Full, conscious and active participation' in liturgy is what the Church desires for all the faithful (*Sacrosanctum Concilium* 2.14), and where children are concerned every help must be given them to bring this about.

Where do we begin?

Jesus began with a bowl of water and a towel, when he washed the feet of his disciples.

He began with bread and wine when he shared a meal with them.

We begin in the same way, with the stuff of everyday life, with everyday human actions and values: doing things as a group, greeting and welcoming, listening, thanking, asking forgiveness, sharing, marking special occasions, experiencing symbolic actions.

Before we can approach liturgy with children we need to have a clear understanding of our own about what liturgy is.

In it we are reborn, nourished, reconciled, healed.

It gives us our priesthood, blesses those who marry and accompanies us throughout life until our journey's end.

Liturgy is what holds us together as a community, is the way in which we express our belief, is what forms us into a community.

In liturgy everything in our lives, everything that makes up our lives is gathered into God and blessed, as God blessed the new creation. All that God made is beautiful and gives God praise, even our sin draws God to us to forgive us.

*At every moment everything in our lives
    is gathered into God.
God is in every activity
    in which we are involved.*

*God is in each word and thought,
    each word I write.
God is at the tip of my paint brush,
    at the point of my pen.
God is in my heart.*

Liturgy is not like the icing on the cake, it is not superimposed, it is already there, woven through the very fabric of our lives. What we are trying to do is to be more aware of God's blessing in our lives, God at work in our lives, and celebrate it.

In liturgy, the baptised share in the priesthood of Christ who has given us an example so that we may copy.

Jesus showed how perfect his love was by getting up from the table, wrapping a towel round his waist, taking a bowl of water and, kneeling before his disciples, washing their feet. This is what liturgy is, perfect love.

The best way to help children to understand the Liturgy of the Mass is to ensure that they have opportunities to experience and appreciate the human values involved in the celebration of the Mass which arise naturally in daily life:

- Helping others
- Working together
- Playing together
- Giving and sharing
- Exchanging greetings
- Listening
- Saying sorry and thank you
- Celebrating

HELPING CHILDREN TO UNDERSTAND AND CELEBRATE THE LITURGY OF THE MASS _____

An overview

It is essential to understand and know what the shape of the Mass, or in fact of any liturgy, is before we can begin to plan with children.

Two great liturgies, Word and Eucharist, form the action of the Mass. These liturgies do not begin and end abruptly – they are preceded by introductory and preparatory rites. A good knowledge of these rites is essential and they need to be explained to the children.

In the Gospels we read how Jesus went to the synagogue on the Sabbath day as he usually did. He stood up to read and they handed him the scroll of the prophet Isaiah (Luke 4: 16-17).

The Sabbath ritual of the Jews was built around the reading of their story.

Jesus frequently shared meals with friends according to the Jewish custom of gathering for a table ritual – a ritual of setting the table, bringing bread and wine and offering prayers of thanksgiving.

Little has changed; we still set the table, place gifts of bread and wine upon it, offer prayers of thanksgiving and recall the words spoken by Jesus.

Gradually the early Church brought together the synagogue ritual and the table ritual to give us what we now call 'The Mass': Word and Eucharist.

Rites

Rites introducing the Liturgy of the Word and the Liturgy of the Eucharist:
- *move people into the right place at the right time*
- *prepare them for what is about to happen*
- *focus them.*

STRUCTURE OF THE MASS _____

Introductory or Opening Rites

Procession and song
Sign of the Cross
Greeting
Penitential Rite
Gloria
Opening Prayer

Liturgy of the Word

First Reading
Responsorial Psalm
Second Reading
Gospel Acclamation
The Gospel
Homily
Profession of Faith
General Intercessions

Liturgy of the Eucharist

Preparation of the Altar
Procession with gifts, and song
Prayers over the bread and wine
Mingling of water and wine
Washing of celebrant's hands
Prayer over the gifts and invitatory dialogue

Eucharistic Prayer

Introductory Dialogue
Preface/Thanksgiving
Holy, holy
Prayer for the Church
Prayer for the Living
Prayer to honour the Saints
Epiclesis/Invocation of the Holy Spirit
Institution narrative and Consecration
Memorial Acclamation
Anamnesis
Elevation/raising up of the consecrated bread and wine
Intercessions for the Church
Final Doxology and Great Amen

The Communion Rite

The Lord's Prayer
Prayer for Peace
Doxology
Rite of Peace
Rite of the Breaking of Bread
Commingling of the Bread and Wine
Lamb of God Litany
Preparation for Communion
Invitaton to Communion
Priest's Communion
Communion Procession and Song
People's Communion
Silent prayer/song of praise
Prayer after Communion

Concluding Rites

Greeting
Blessing
Dismissal
Recessional Procession

When celebrating Masses with children it is permissible to omit certain elements. The following, however must always be included:
One introductory element
Opening prayer
The Gospel Reading
Liturgy of the Eucharist
Eucharistic Prayer (Eucharistic Prayers for use with children are available)
Communion Rite
Concluding Rite
(See Directory of Children's Masses, Chapter 3.)

INTRODUCTORY OR OPENING RITES _____

Purpose

A call to worship. To gather those assembled into a celebrating community leading to an awareness of the presence of God who has assembled, not a group of individuals who have come together to express themselves, but a community of faith who have come together to prepare for the reading of the scriptures and the breaking of bread.

Structure	Purpose
Procession and song	Moves the assembly into the celebration, unites them as a community and highlights the purpose of the gathering.
Sign of the Cross	Calls upon the Blessed Trinity and reminds the community that they worship together as people Baptised in the name of the Father, Son and Holy Spirit.
Greeting	Joyfully recognises Christ present among his people gathered for prayer.
Penitential Rite	To profess faith in the loving mercy of God who constantly forgives us in Christ.
Gloria	Song to praise God.
Opening Prayer	Gathers the silent prayer of the community into the spoken prayer of the celebrant expressing the theme of the celebration, and addresses the petition to God the Father through Christ and the Holy Spirit.

LITURGY OF THE WORD

Purpose

To proclaim the good news of salvation and reveal God to the people.

Structure	Purpose
First Reading	Usually a reading from the Old Testament reminding the community of the wonderful works of God among the people of the Old Testament.
Responsorial Psalm	To respond to God's word by using God's word.
Second Reading	This reading is taken from the New Testament, except the Gospel. Read on Sundays and certain feasts.
Gospel Acclamation	A joyful shout of anticipation and readiness to welcome what is to come.
The Gospel	Christ speaks.
Homily	Unfolds the mystery of Christ proclaimed in the scriptures and applies God's word to the needs and circumstances of life today.
Profession of Faith	The community assents to the Word and homily and calls to mind the truths of Faith before celebrating the Eucharist.
General Intercessions	Invitations to pray for intentions announced.

The proclamation of the Word is central to the life of the community. It is a story, not of past events, but an experience of the living God revealing himself to his people today.

When the Word is proclaimed in a liturgical assembly God speaks to his people and Christ proclaims his good news.

The ambo, or table of the Word, represents the dignity and uniqueness of God's Word and is afforded the same reverence and respect as the altar, the table of the Lord.

The appearance and presentation of the book from which the Word of God is read is important as it helps children to approach the Word of God with dignity and respect.

The book may be enhanced by making an attractive cover for it, or even several covers for the Liturgical seasons of the Church's year, feast days and other special occasions.

It is not easy to read the Bible aloud therefore great care must be given to the choice and preparation of readers who are not speaking their own words but the Word of God. No one benefits when a reading is inaudible and the Word is lost.

Attention to these details help to foster respect and reverence in the children towards the Word of God and they can gradually take on the responsibility for the presentation of the 'Book' and the preparation of the table of the Word.

When celebrating a Liturgy of the Word with children a table of the Word can be prepared with a special stand or cushion on which to place the 'Book of the Word'.

Other items on the table of the Word can represent the Liturgical season being celebrated, the feast day or special occasion.

First Reading

Usually taken from the Old Testament, the first reading reminds the community of God's everlasting love and wonderful works among the people of the Old Testament.

The Bible is a treasure trove of stories about people, places, events, poetry, law, prophecy and wisdom. Good people and bad, wise people and foolish, rich and poor and the wonderful works of God among them. But it is important to remember that all the stories are part of the larger on-going story of salvation and the wonder of the revelation of God's everlasting love.

Responsorial Psalm

A psalm is a song and a prayer, many of which were composed by King David.

The Responsorial Psalm is what its name tells us, a psalm of response by which the community greets the Word of God to which they have just listened.

God has spoken and we answer with thanksgiving and praise.

As far as possible everyone participates in the singing or recitation of the psalm.

Second Reading

This is a New Testament reading. It is usually omitted in Masses celebrated with children.

Gospel Acclamation

Alleluia: *hallelu* praise, and *Yah* Yahweh – Praise God.
Of all the rites connected with the Liturgy of the Word the reverence due to the Gospel reading requires special attention.

This is a sung acclamation. If it is not sung it is replaced by a short time of silence. The community stands to acclaim the coming of the Lord present in his word.

The Gospel

The Book of the Gospels remains on the altar until the minister takes it to the lectern accompanied by acolytes carrying lighted candles.

The Gospel is the only reading traditionally accompanied by a procession and other signs of honour which emphasise the presence of Christ in his word.

The minister of the Gospel greets the community with the words: 'The Lord be with you,' to which all reply: 'And also with you.' At the same time the triple sign of the cross is made on the forehead, lips and heart expressing the desire that our minds be receptive to the word of Christ, our lips speak it and our hearts love it. At the conclusion of the Gospel the minister proclaims: 'This is the Gospel of the Lord,' to which all reply: 'Praise to you, Lord Jesus Christ.'

Homily

The homily develops some point from the readings of the Mass of the day and suggests a link between the Word and daily living.

The Homily is usually given by an ordained minister. But in Masses with children the Homily may sometimes take the form of a dialogue or be given by another person.

Profession of Faith

By reciting the Creed, the rule of faith, together with our fellow Christians we identify ourselves with the faith of the Church. We are reminded that we are members of the community of the Baptised. The people to whom God says: 'I have called you by name, I love you,' to which we reply: 'I believe you love me.'

General Intercessions

General Intercessions or Prayer of the Faithful invites the community to use their priestly powers to pray for all humankind. This prayer gathers the whole world into the Eucharist.

The intercessions are an invitation to those gathered to open their hearts as wide as the heart of Christ who in love died for all people.

These prayers normally take the form of intention and response, rather like a litany, which the celebrant draws to a conclusion with a short prayer asking God to look with favour on our prayer which we make through Jesus Christ our Lord.

LITURGY OF THE EUCHARIST

Preparation Rites

Purpose
To prepare the altar and the community for what is to come.
A ritual setting aside of gifts expressive of ourselves.
With a joyful heart the community prepares to give to God what God first gave to them.

Structure	Purpose
Preparation of the altar	To set the table with altar cloth, candles, corporal, purificator, chalice, missal.
Procession with gifts, and song	To bring gifts expressive of the life of the community for the liturgy (bread, wine, money) to the table.
Prayers over the bread and wine	Focuses attention on the bread and wine, symbols of our life and work, and praises God in the continuing work of creation. A promise of transformation of the gifts to a new level of existence. They will become for us the bread of life and spiritual drink.
Mingling of water and wine	Symbolic purpose.
Washing of celebrant's hands	A practical action in former times.
Prayer over the gifts and invitatory dialogue	Look forward to the Eucharistic prayer.

Preparation Rites

Using the term 'preparation of the altar and gifts' describes what we previously called the offertory. The community now prepares to celebrate the liturgy of the Eucharist and sets the table, the Lord's table, which is the centre of the Eucharistic liturgy.

This is a functional activity not to be prolonged.

Procession with gifts, and song

Gifts of bread and wine are brought forward in procession from the body of the community, a reminder that in earlier times it was the custom for people to bring bread and wine from their homes for the Eucharist.

Accepted by the priest, the gifts are placed on the altar. This is the first stage of the journey of the bread and wine which will be completed in the distribution of Communion.

Water is not presented nor is the chalice, but gifts appropriate to the occasion may be presented. (For example, gifts to meet the needs of the Church and the poor.)

This procession, a symbolic action and representing the movement of the community, should take place with dignity and with attention paid to the way the gifts are carried.

Joyful instrumental music, a short hymn, or a choral piece may accompany the procession.

Other gifts brought forward in this procession should precede the bread and wine, for example, gifts for the poor as in the Holy Thursday liturgy, but should not overwhelm the bread and wine which are the only gifts placed on the altar.

Prayers over the bread and wine

At the Last Supper, Jesus took some bread into his hands and said the blessing; then he took the cup and gave thanks to God.

Like the traditional Jewish meal our meal now begins with a blessing as we remember that everything we are, everything we have, everything we do comes from God.

'Blessed are you, Lord God of all creation.
Through your goodness we have this bread to offer,
which earth has given and human hands have made.
It will become for us the bread of life.'

God is blessed for his goodness in creating us to work with him and is recognised as the source of all being. As priestly people, baptised in Christ, we offer all creation and all human kind to be saved and reconciled to God in Christ.

The bread and wine held up by the priest, symbols of our life and work on earth, will be transformed by the power of the Holy Spirit. Our lives will be transformed into a new level of existence nourished by the bread of life and our spiritual drink.

Prayer over the gifts and invitatory dialogue

Extending his hands, the celebrant invites the community to join in praying that the gifts offered may be acceptable to God and spiritually benefit the community.

'Pray brethren that our sacrifice may be acceptable to God, the almighty Father.'

THE EUCHARISTIC PRAYER _____

Purpose

Transformation of the whole assembly.

Structure	Purpose
Introductory Dialogue	An invitation for the community to lift up their hearts to God and enter into the Eucharistic prayer.
Preface/Thanksgiving	Proclamation of thanksgiving and praise in the name of the people of God. Earth unites with heaven to sing the new song of creation.
Acclamation/Holy, holy	An acclamation inspired by the vision of Isaiah (Isaiah 6:2-3). Joining with the angels it is sung by the whole community.
Prayer for the Church	
Prayer for the Living	
Prayer to honour the Saints	

Epiclesis/Invocation of the Holy Spirit	Prayer that the Holy Spirit may come and transform not only the bread and wine but the whole community.
Narrative of Institution/ Consecration	Makes present the total mystery of the death, resurrection and glorification of Christ.
Memorial Acclamation	The community proclaims the Mystery of Faith.
Anamnesis	Fulfils Christ's command 'Do this in memory of me.' The community remembers and makes Christ's offering its own.
Intercessions for the Church	

Final Doxology and   Everyone present acclaims in a loud voice, 'Amen.'
Great Amen   – 'So be it.'

The Eucharistic Prayer is the great prayer of praise and thanksgiving extolling God's wonderful works and marvellous deeds among his people. It has its origins in Judaism where it was customary to use prayers of this kind on both public and private occasions, for example the Passover meal. At the Last Supper Jesus prayed in this way.

The Eucharist is:

- the sacrament of our salvation which Christ accomplished on the cross
- the sacrifice of praise and thanksgiving for the work of creation, redemption and sanctification
- the sacrifice of praise by which the Church, in the name of everything created, sings the glory of God
- the sacrifice made possible only through Christ who unites the faithful to himself, to his praise, to his prayer, to his sacrifice
- the sacrifice of praise offered to God through Christ, with Christ and in Christ (CCC 1359).

Four Eucharistic Prayers for use in the Roman Liturgy are to be found in the missal. In addition there are special Eucharistic Prayers for Masses with children, reconciliation Masses and for use on certain other occasions.

Introductory Dialogue

The community rise to their feet for this solemn beginning of the Eucharistic Prayer.

Celebrant and community are reminded that the Lord is present with them. 'The Lord be with you', they lift up their hearts and to the Lord and give him thanks and praise.

It is more appropriate to sing the Preface and this includes the introductory dialogue.

Preface/Thanksgiving

This great song of thanksgiving is sung by the priest with arms extended and embracing everyone present.

A choice of 80 texts is available for this great song in which the Church gives thanks to God the Father, Son and Holy Spirit, for the works of creation, redemption and sanctification, joining the unending praise of the angels and saints.

Acclamation/Holy, holy

It is composed of four biblical acclamations:

Holy, holy, holy Lord,
God of power and might –

Heaven and earth are full of your glory –

Hosanna in the highest.

Blessed is he who comes in the name of the Lord.
Hosanna in the highest.

The Holy, holy, or Sanctus, is the most important prayer in the Eucharistic liturgy and if nothing else can be sung this is the one hymn which should be sung at every Mass.

Prayer for the Church – for the Living – to honour the Saints

These prayers are included before the Institution narrative only in Eucharistic Prayer Rite 1.

Prayer for the Church

We ask God to watch over, guide and grant peace and unity to the Church throughout the world.

Prayer for the Living

We are invited to mention by name those for whom we wish to pray. We ask the Lord to remember all the people present who believe in God, people dedicated to God, people offering this sacrifice of praise for themselves and for all those they love. Asking God to be mindful for their well-being and redemption.

Prayer to honour the Saints

We join with the whole Church to honour Mary, the virgin Mother of Jesus Christ our Lord and God, St Joseph, her husband and the apostles and martyrs whose names are listed. Rather like a roll-call.

Saints connected with the school or church, or name saints or saints on their feast days can be included in the list. We ask that their merits and prayers will help and protect us always.

Epiclesis/Invocation of the Holy Spirit

During the invocation of the Holy Spirit the priest places his hands over the bread and wine and asks that the Holy Spirit may come and make the offerings of bread and wine holy so that they will be changed into the Lord's body and blood.

Narrative of Institution/The Lord's Supper and Consecration

The sacrifice which Christ instituted at the Last Supper is celebrated in the words and actions of Christ when he offered his body and blood under the appearances of bread and wine.

A moment before the consecration it is permissible to ring a bell as a sign of attention and reverence, also at the elevation of the consecrated bread and the elevation of the consecrated wine.

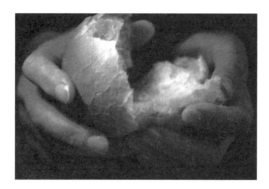

'Take this all of you and eat it: this is my body which will be given up for you.'

Each Consecration narrative used in the four Eucharistic Prayers has its own introduction.
1. The day before he suffered . . .
2. Before he was given up to death . . .
3. On the night he was betrayed . . .
4. He always loved those who were his own in the world . . .

Mystery of Faith/Memorial Acclamation

Immediately after the Institution narrative the community is invited to proclaim the mystery of faith. The total mystery of Christ is present and active now among his people who wait for him to come again in glory.

All is accomplished by Christ, but all is still in the process of being accomplished in the people of God on earth.

*Christ **has** died,*
*Christ **is** risen,*
*Christ **will** come again.*

29

Anamnesis

People and ministers gathered in union with the whole Church remember the passion, resurrection and ascension of Christ and offer to God this holy and perfect sacrifice. The greatest of all the many gifts given to us by God.

They ask God to accept their offerings as he once accepted the gifts of Abel, Abraham and Melchizedek.

They pray for God's angel to take this sacrifice to God's table in heaven.

They pray to be filled with every grace and blessing when they receive from this altar the sacred body and blood of the Son of God.

Intercessions for the Church

These intercessions remind us that we celebrate the Eucharist in communion with the whole Church in heaven and on earth and that the sacrifice of Christ's body and blood is offered for all the members of the Church, living and dead.

They are presented in the form of a litany –
Lord, remember your Church throughout the world.
May we grow in love together with our pope (*N*), bishop (*N*), clergy (*N*).

Lord, remember our brothers and sisters who have died.
May they rest in the peace of Christ.

Make us worthy to share eternal life with Mary, the Mother of God, the apostles (*N*), the saints (*N*).

May we sing your glory together with them for ever and ever through Christ our Lord.

Final Doxology and Great Amen

Through him, with him, in him, in the unity of the Holy Spirit,
all honour and glory is yours, almighty Father, for ever and ever. AMEN.

THE COMMUNION RITE _____

Structure	Purpose
The Lord's Prayer	Petitions for daily needs, Eucharistic bread, the deliverance of the community from the powers of evil and peace on earth. Prayer of preparation for Communion.
Prayer for Peace	An extension of the last petition of the Lord's Prayer is said by the celebrant for deliverance from evil and for perfect peace.
Doxology	For the kingdom, the power and the glory are yours now and for ever. The people gathered give assent to the prayer. Amen.
Rite of Peace	For the community to share and pray for peace before sharing the one bread. It is the Lord's Prayer in action and a witness of what it means to be a Eucharistic community. Before sharing the one bread the community prays for peace and unity for the Church and for the whole human family and offer a sign of their love for one another.
Rite of the Breaking of Bread	A sign that in sharing the one bread we are one body in Christ.
Commingling of the Bread and Wine	A small particle of bread is put into the wine.
Lamb of God Litany	A litany sung during the breaking of the bread.
Preparation for Communion	Celebrant and people prepare privately for Communion.
Invitation to Communion	This is the Lamb of God, the Eucharistic bread is shown to the community.
Priest's Communion	The Celebrant receives the Body and Blood of Christ.
Communion procession and song	The community as members of one body process together to the table of the Lord, united in song.

Profession of Faith/ People's Communion	'Amen' triple profession of faith.
Silent prayer after Communion	The community reflects silently on Christ's power transforming them as they continue his transforming work in the world.
Song of Praise	A song of praise may be sung.
Prayer after Communion	The celebrant invites the people to pray that the Eucharist will have its effect in their lives and bring them into God's kingdom.

The Lord's Prayer

From earliest times the Lord's Prayer has been included in the liturgy preparatory to the sharing of Christ's body and blood. It is the prayer to the Father taught to us by Jesus and is a summary of the whole Gospel.

In it we name our hearts' desires:

- that God be honoured
- that the kingdom comes
- that God's will be done
- that we are given our daily bread
- that we are forgiven, that we forgive
- that we are not led into temptation
- that we are delivered from evil.

The celebrant offers the invitation to pray and all unite in praying this prayer aloud.

'Let us pray with confidence to the Father in the words our Saviour gave us.'

Rite of Peace

Before sharing the same bread the community prays for peace for the Church and for the whole human family:

Lord Jesus Christ, you said to your apostles: 'I leave you my peace, my peace I give you.' Look not on our sins but on the faith of your Church, and grant us the peace and unity of your kingdom where you live for ever and ever. Amen.

The celebrant gives the greeting of peace and invites the community to show some sign of love for one another.

Unobtrusive music may accompany the sign of peace leading to the Lamb of God. It is not appropriate to sing a hymn at this point, not even on the theme of peace.

Rite of the Breaking of Bread

In the early Church one large loaf of unleavened bread was broken and distributed. Not only is the breaking of bread the most primitive rite of preparation for communion, it is the most powerful symbol of the oneness of the community. The repetition of this action of Christ at the Last Supper was considered so important to the celebration of the Eucharist that the Mass was called 'the breaking of bread'.

'We, though many, are one body, all of us who partake of the one bread.' 1 Corinthians 10:17

Commingling of the Bread and Wine

The commingling takes place as a sign that the fullness of the eucharistic presence resides completely in either bread or wine – they are not two separate eucharistic presences.

Lamb of God Litany

The singing of the 'Lamb of God' accompanies the breaking of bread and continues for as long as needed.

Preparation for Communion

This is the time when the celebrant prays silently in preparation for Communion. The community should do the same.

This should be a marked time of silence in the Mass. Children can be guided in how to pray at this time and be taught prayers asking to benefit from receiving the body and blood of Jesus.

Invitation to Communion

Lifting up the consecrated bread the celebrant shows it to the people while saying the words:
    'This is the Lamb of God', inviting all to share in the Eucharistic banquet.

The community responds with the words:
    'Lord, I am not worthy to receive you but only say the word and I shall be healed.'

Communion procession and song

The act of Communion is a community action.
    By receiving communion the community fully participates in the celebration of the Eucharist according to our Lord's command:
    'Take it and eat; this is my body . . . All of you drink of this; this is my blood of the New Covenant, which is poured out for many for the forgiveness of sins.' Matthew 26:26-27

In earlier liturgies the communion ritual was celebrated in a festive setting, during a meal at which Christian families gathered to celebrate Jesus Christ. The communion song therefore expresses the joy of an encounter with the Lord. The community singing together in the communion procession emphasises oneness in Christ.

Profession of Faith/People's Communion

The Minister of communion holds the consecrated bread before each communicant and says 'the Body of Christ' to which the communicant responds 'Amen' and receives the bread from the minister.

When distributing from the cup the minister says 'the Blood of Christ' to which the communicant responds 'Amen' then takes the cup from the minister and drinks a little of the consecrated wine.

The 'Amen' is not a 'thank you' but a profession of faith in:

• the presence of Christ in the community

• the presence of Christ in the communicant

• the presence of Christ under the forms of bread and wine.

To receive communion in the hand rest one hand upon the other palm up. The communicant steps to one side and places the bread in their mouth before moving off to their place.

Silent Prayer/Song of Praise

A short time of silence may follow communion or a song of praise may be sung.

A litany of praise and thanksgiving may be used instead of a song. A reader may recite or a cantor sing the invocations to which all respond.

The invocations are not petitions but statements of praise and thanksgiving. For the gift of . . . let us praise the Lord.

Prayer after Communion

In the prayer after communion the gifts of the Eucharist are recalled and the celebrant prays that they may bear fruit in the lives of the community.

CONCLUDING RITES

Purpose

To say farewell until we meet again.

Structure	Purpose
Final Greeting	To greet the community for the final time.
Blessing	To ask in the name of the Trinity for the power of God to come upon the community.
Dismissal	To send the community forth to praise God and do good works.
The recessional procession	Functional.

Final Greeting

With arms outstretched the celebrant greets the community for the final time.

'The Lord be with you.'

Blessing

The celebrant calls upon the Trinity and asks for God's power to descend upon the community.

The blessing may be given in simple or solemn form.

Solemn blessings are given for certain times of the Church's year and some feast days. When a solemn blessing is given the people are asked to bow their heads and pray for God's blessing. To each of the three parts of the blessing the response, Amen, *is made and again after the blessing.*

Dismissal

The traditional Roman dismissal text *Ite missa est* quite literally meant, 'Go, it is over'.

The community is sent forth in the peace of Christ to live what they have just celebrated.

The Recessional Procession

The celebrant and ministers leave the assembly. A hymn may be sung but it is not part of the liturgy.

The recessional procession sometimes mirrors the entrance procession: the reader carrying the book of the Gospels; a server carrying the cross; acolytes, etc.

This procession serves a functional purpose and should not be prolonged.

CELEBRATING WITH CHILDREN

Celebrations which help children to understand some of the elements of liturgy are important for their liturgical formation and help them to participate more fully in the liturgical life of the Church. Such celebrations can take place in the classroom, in year groups, in whole school assemblies, in church groups or services.

For example, preparing for a Christmas celebration poses no problems. From birth, almost, children know how to prepare and decorate for Christmas. They will happily co-operate in making paper chains and sending out Christmas cards. Again, when Halloween comes along their imaginations are full of wonderful ideas and need little encouragement, and birthday celebrations come naturally. It is these natural tendencies which are drawn on in the preparation and celebration of liturgy.

Giving children opportunities to use their natural skills and talents to minister in liturgy is not only beneficial for the child, but for the whole Church.

Ministries

- The preparation of the worship space in which the community gathers is a ministry.

- The ministry of music is obvious, either singing as a community, choir or solo and playing instruments.

- Reading is a very important ministry. Readers must prepare well and read audibly, clearly and with reverence and understanding of what they are reading.

- Art is also a valuable ministry in liturgy. Through art children can enhance the liturgical environment with flower arrangements, banners, altar frontals. They can prepare invitations and leaflets.

- Drama, dance and mime can be a very effective way of involving children in the liturgy, aiding concentration and prayer by providing a focus, and drawing out the meaning of scripture or a particular movement of the Mass.

- The ministry of welcome and hospitality is key to creating the atmosphere of community. Ushers too may be required.

- Procession of gifts needs gift bearers to present the offerings on behalf of the community.
- The ministry of altar serving is to be encouraged.
- Confirmed children may also be eligible for the ministry of the distribution of Communion but must be commissioned by the approved Diocesan authority.

THE CHURCH'S YEAR

Beginning with the first Sunday of Advent until its close with the celebration of the Kingship of Christ, the year of the Church is filled with wonderful seasons and feasts to celebrate – Advent, Christmas, Epiphany, Lent, Easter, Pentecost, Trinity, Candlemas, Feasts of Our Lord and Our Lady and numerous saints. In addition there are also celebrations particular to a school or group or parish.

Whenever possible liturgy with children should follow the calendar of the Church's year.

The Year of the Church (The Lord's Year of Grace) is made up of 52 weeks which are divided into five seasons: Advent, Christmastide, Ordinary time, Lent and Eastertide.

Advent has four weeks, Christmastide two weeks.
Lent has six weeks, Eastertide seven weeks and Ordinary time has the remaining 33 weeks.
Ordinary time begins after Christmastide, breaks for Lent and Eastertide and resumes again after Eastertide (Pentecost).
The number of weeks of Ordinary time between Christmastide and Lent varies according to the date of Easter Sunday and likewise when this season resumes after Eastertide.

Older children might be encouraged to make their own 'Lord's Year of Grace' calendars including in them their own special days: birthday, baptism, First Communion, significant feast days . . .

Each season of the Church has its own liturgical colour:
Advent – mauve
Christmastide – white
Lent – purple
Eastertide – white
Ordinary time – green
Pentecost Sunday – red.

These colours can be used to colour the seasons on the calendar.

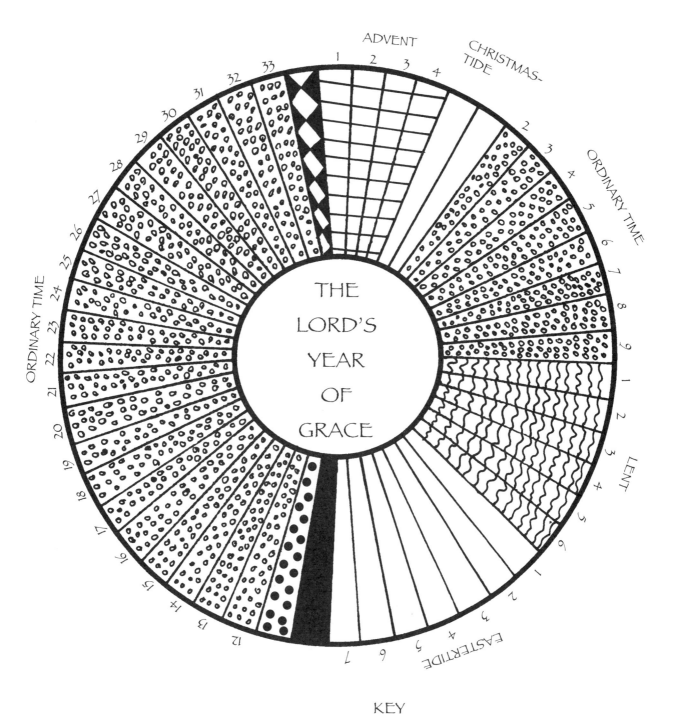

KEY

MAUVE		ADVENT
WHITE		CHRISTMASTIDE
PURPLE		LENT
WHITE		EASTERTIDE
GREEN		ORDINARY TIME
RED		PENTECOST
		TRINITY SUNDAY
		CHRIST THE KING

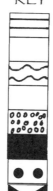

CO-OPERATING AS A COMMUNITY

Preparation of the space

The purpose of the occasion to be celebrated will decide the place of celebration, the arrangement and the use of the space, and the decor and the allocation of responsibilities or 'ministries'.

- Where is the celebration to be held?
- What atmosphere needs to be created?
- In what ways can the space be arranged to meet the needs of the celebration?
- Who will do this?
- Into what kind of a place are those coming to celebrate welcomed?
- How are they welcomed? By whom?
- What does the atmosphere encourage?

Groups of children can take turns to be responsible for:
- creating a focal point, deciding the best place for it and how they will make it. . .
- how the seating will be arranged . . . will it be in straight rows facing the focal point or around it or more informally?
- placement of artefacts, children's work, etc.
- how those gathering will be welcomed.

Gathering

Structure	Purpose
Procession and song	Moves the assembly into the celebration,
Sign of the Cross	unites them as a community,
Greeting	highlights the purpose of the gathering.

Procession and song

Arrange how the group celebrating will move into the celebration:
- Will there be a procession?
- Where will the procession begin? Where will it end?
- Who will be in it?
- Who starts it off?
- Will it be accompanied by music/singing?
- Will anything be carried in the procession?
- From where will these items be collected?

- Where will they be carried to?
- Who will receive them?
- Where are they to be placed?
- Where do the processors then go?

Children already in the room may be gathered with one or two of the following:

- a moment of silence, or music, or a hymn, or song, or symbolic movement
- placing posters or artefacts in the focal point
- a short reading or introduction on the theme of the gathering.

The Sign of the Cross

Calls upon the Blessed Trinity and reminds us that we worship together as people Baptised in the name of the Father, Son and Holy Spirit.

The Sign of the Cross can be extended:
In the name of God our loving Father,
in the name of Jesus, God's beloved Son,
in the name of the Holy Spirit, sent to teach us the way to heaven.
or
In the name of God who made us,
in the name of Jesus who saves us,
in the name of the Holy Spirit who guides us on our way.

Children can compose their own Sign of the Cross.

Greeting

The greeting is a joyful recognition of Christ present with us.

Children and teachers/catechists welcome each other to the new day with a simple greeting, for example: 'Good morning, it is good to see everyone again,' and acknowledge those absent, pray for the sick and for the needs of the day.

CELEBRATION BASED ON THE GATHERING RITE OF THE MASS

Theme: FRIENDSHIP

Preparation

Prepare the space and focal point
In the focal point place:
- a stand-up card with the word FRIENDSHIP printed in large letters
- an individual 'friendship is . . .' card prepared by each child.

Gathering

Gather the group by reading some of the children's 'friendship is . . .' cards.

Leader We gather to pray: In the name of God our loving Father,
in the name of Jesus, God's beloved Son,
in the name of the Holy Spirit, who makes us one.

Invite the reading of more friendship cards.
Pause for a few moments of silent reflection . . .
How we can show friendship in our lives today?

Let us show friendship to those in need of our prayers.
Invite children to name the people for whom they want to pray.
   Respond to each naming by singing: 'When I needed a neighbour were you there . . .' *(refrain only).*

Prayer

Leader Let us pray that God will help us to grow in love for one another . . .
(Prayer composed by the pupils thanking God for friends, for the ways in which friends have helped them, for God's help to be good friends to others.)
. . .We make our prayer through Jesus Christ, our Lord. Amen.

Lent

During Lent a Penitential Rite could be included in the prayer and the nature of this gathering would be reflected in the focal point, gathering music, hymn or reading, and other artefacts. The Sign of the Cross can be specially composed by a group of children.

We greet each other in the name of Jesus who waits to forgive us our sins:
    'May the Lord be with us, the love of God and the peace of the Holy Spirit as we come to ask for forgiveness.'

CELEBRATION BASED ON THE PENITENTIAL RITE OF THE MASS

RITE 1: THE 'I CONFESS'

Preparation

Prepare the space and focal point.
In the focal point place:
- pictures or statues of Jesus, Our Lady, angels, saints
- individual cards or one large card with the names of everyone present.

Gathering

Play peaceful music to gather the group.

Leader   We gather together today in the name of God the Father who made us,
and of Jesus, Son of God, who died to save us,
and of the Holy Spirit, always with us, as we come to pray for forgiveness.
Let us greet the persons next to us with the words . . .
'The peace of Christ be with you.'

Let us remember in our hearts a time when perhaps we did not greet someone with the peace of Christ but with unkindness.

We pray now for forgiveness:

All pray the Confiteor together from the text as printed out below.

I confess to Almighty God,
and to you my brothers and sisters
that I have sinned through my own fault
in my thoughts . . . *(pause)*
and in my words . . . *(pause)*
in what I have done . . . *(pause)*
and in what I have failed to do . . .*(pause)*
and I ask blessed Mary, ever virgin,
all the angels and saints *(especially school or church patron or saint of the day),*
and you, my brothers and sisters,
to pray for me to the Lord our God.
Lord in your mercy hear our prayer for:
(Names from the focal point can be read out in litany form.)

Prayer

Let us pray that God will help us to grow in love for one another . . .
(A short prayer of thanksgiving, which the children can help to compose and pray either individually or with a partner, can conclude this celebration.)
. . .We make our prayer through Jesus Christ, our Lord. Amen.

RITE 2: THE LORD HAVE MERCY

Lord, we have sinned against you: *(pause)*
(Each one present may speak their name.)
Lord have mercy.

Lord, show us your mercy and love.
And grant us your salvation.

RITE 3: LORD, HAVE MERCY; CHRIST, HAVE MERCY . . .

Lord, you were sent to heal the sorrowful:
Lord, have mercy. **R** Lord, have mercy.

Lord, you came to call sinners:
Christ, have mercy. **R** Christ, have mercy.

Lord, you plead for our forgiveness at the right hand of the Father.
Lord, have mercy. **R** Lord, have mercy.

This form of the penitential rite has many musical settings which can be used with the children. It can also be accompanied with symbolic movement.

First petition: recited or sung while kneeling with hands joined and heads bowed.

Second petition: move to kneeling on one knee with hands open and arms outstretched at shoulder level.

Third petition: move to full standing position with arms fully raised above head – end by slowly lowering arms to sides.

The invocations can be changed but the responses, 'Lord, have mercy; Christ, have mercy,' always remain the same. The children can be helped to compose their own invocations – remembering that this is not an examination of conscience, but a prayer for forgiveness in joyful recognition of the saving presence of the risen Christ among us.

SONG OF PRAISE – THE GLORIA _____

The Gloria can be included in liturgies with children to mark special occasions, for example Eastertide, feast days, the completion of a piece of work, success, birthdays or groups of birthdays, good news.

It has many musical settings which the children can learn and they can also accompany it with percussion, symbolic movement or dance. It can be sung or recited by alternating groups or individuals.

Suggestion

Voice or group of voices

1   Glory to God in the highest *(arms raised high)*

2   and peace to his people on earth. *(arms stretched forward, palms up)*

3   Lord God, heavenly king, *(arms raised high)*

4   almighty God and Father. *(arms raised high)*

All   We worship you. *(hands joined, heads bowed)*

All   We give you thanks. *(hands joined, heads raised)*

All   We praise you for your glory. *(arms raised high)*

1   Lord Jesus Christ, *(one child holds up a crucifix)*
only Son of the Father,

2   Lord God, Lamb of God, you take away the sins of the world:

All   have mercy on us. *(bow from waist)*

3   You are seated at the right hand of the Father;

All   receive our prayer. *(hands joined, heads raised)*

4   For you alone are the Holy one. *(arms raised high to end)*

All   You alone are the Lord, you alone are the Most High,
Jesus Christ, with the Holy Spirit in the glory of God the Father.
AMEN. *(lower arms and join hands at waist level)*

INVITATION TO PRAY

Opening Prayer

Gathers the silent prayer of the community into the spoken prayer of the celebrant expressing the theme of the celebration.

This prayer has four elements:

- invitation to pray
- brief moment of silence
- spoken prayer, addressed to God the Father through Christ in the Holy Spirit
- acclamation 'Amen' assent of the people.

For liturgy with children they can be helped to compose a prayer for use by the group either for the week or daily or special prayers for occasions based on the theme of a special celebration – remembering that this prayer is the prayer of those gathered and is always made in the name of Jesus Christ, our Lord.

Before this prayer is prayed all are invited to spend a few moments in silence, aware that they are in God's presence and recalling what they wish to pray for.

During this prayer the children can be encouraged to hold their hands in the 'Orans' extended position like a priest does when praying this prayer, reminding us that it is addressed to God.

Example

Let us pray:
Almighty and ever-loving God,
    who gives us each day our daily bread,
help us always to follow Christ our Lord faithfully
    and do your will here on earth.
We ask this through Our Lord Jesus Christ, your Son,
    who lives and reigns with you and the Holy Spirit,
    one God, for ever and ever. Amen.

CELEBRATION BASED ON THE LITURGY OF THE WORD USING AN OLD TESTAMENT READING

Theme: FRIENDSHIP (1 Samuel 19:1-7)

Preparation

Prepare the space and focal point.

The focal point will be the table of the Word with a place for:
- the Book of the Word; for example, a cushion or a bookrest or cover for the book if needed
- cloth for the table
- candles (if safe)
- flowers.

Posters or artefacts related to the message of the text to be read. For example: pictures of friends who have helped each other, people who have befriended others, etc.

Gathering

Process the Book of the Word into the room and place it on the table of the Word or lift it from the table and process it around the room accompanied by a chant or hymn of praise, for example:

Praise God, praise God, praise God,
praise God in the morning,
praise God in the noontime.
Praise God, praise God, praise God till the sun goes down. (575, *Liturgical Hymns Old and New*, Kevin Mayhew)

Greeting and Introduction

Leader *(A teacher, catechist or child(ren))* Welcomes those assembled and introduces the reading.

Our reading is taken from the First Book of Samuel and tells us about the friendship between two great men, Jonathan, the son of King Saul, and David, once a shepherd boy, who would become a king. In this reading we hear how Jonathan saves the life of David.

Proclaiming the Word

The minister or ministers of the Word walk to the table of the Word and lift up the book. (The reading is done from the book, not from pieces of paper unless these are first placed inside the book.)

R1   Jonathan steps in to help David.

R2   King Saul told Jonathan, his son, and all his servants of his intention to kill David.

R3   Jonathan, Saul's son, had great love and respect for David and so warned him:

R4   'My Father Saul is looking for a way to kill you, so be on your guard tomorrow morning; hide away in some secret place. I will go out and keep my father company in the fields where you are hiding and will talk to my father about you; I will find out what the situation is and let you know.'

R3   So Jonathan spoke well of David to Saul his father:

R4   'Do not let the king sin against his servant David, for David has not sinned against you. Everything he has done has been greatly to your advantage. He risked his life for you when killing the Philistine and God brought about a great victory for all Israel. You saw it yourself and rejoiced; why then sin against innocent blood by killing David without cause?'

R2   King Saul was impressed by Jonathan's words and took an oath:

R5   'As Yahweh lives, I will not kill him.'

R3   Jonathan called David and told him all these things. Then Jonathan brought David to King Saul and David served him as before.

R1   **This is the word of the Lord.**

All   **Thanks be to God.**

Response

Praise God, etc. *Sung response* (575, *Liturgical Hymns Old and New*).

Homily

Invite the pupils to share what they have learned about friendship from this story.

Intercessions

Litany of Friendship.

We thank God for all our friends.

Response

Said.
Praise God, praise God, praise God for the gift of friends.
We thank God for the times our friends have helped us.
Sung response (575, *Liturgical Hymns Old and New*)
We thank God for the times we have been good friends.
Sung response
We pray for the lonely who have no friends, *etc.*
Sung response

Prayer

Almighty and ever-loving God, our greatest friend,
　　we thank you for the gift of friendship.
Help us to be loving and loyal to our friends
　　as Jonathan was to David and as Jesus, your beloved Son, is to us.
We ask this through our Lord Jesus Christ, your Son,
　　who lives and reigns with you and the Holy Spirit,
　　one God for ever and ever. Amen.

CELEBRATION BASED ON A PSALM _____

Theme: PENTECOST

Preparation

Prepare the space and focal point:
- prepare a card with the text: Come Holy Spirit
- decorate the focal point with symbols of the Holy Spirit.

Gathering

Gather the group to a Taizé Holy Spirit chant or hymn to the Holy Spirit.

Greeting and Introduction

Leader We gather today to celebrate the coming of the Holy Spirit.
In the name of the Father and of the Son and of the Holy Spirit.

Psalm 103
Response:
Send forth your Spirit, O Lord, and renew the face of the earth.

The response can be sung first by one voice and then repeated by a group. It can be sung between each verse of the psalm.

All say the psalm
Bless the Lord, my soul!

Facing front, dancer(s) kneel with arms crossed over chest . . . head looking up.

Lord God, how great you are.
Response

Raise arms above head.

How many are your works, O Lord!
The earth is full of your riches.

Bring arms down in a circular movement to waist level at front of body, palms facing upwards.

Response

You take back your Spirit, they die, returning to the dust from which they came.
Response

Stretch arms to the ground, palms facing out. Kneel on one knee and bow low.

You send forth your Spirit, they are created; and you renew the face of the earth. *Response*	*Slowly move to standing position and raise arms above head.*
May the glory of the Lord last for ever! May the Lord rejoice in all his works! *Response*	*Keeping arms extended, lower to shoulder level and turn body around in a circle.*
May my thoughts be pleasing to God. In God I find my joy.	*Bring hands to front of body, join them and raise head up.* *Separate hands and move out and up in a circular movement.*

Response

Prayer

Leader   Let us pray that like the apostles on the first Pentecost day
we will be filled with the power and the gifts of the Holy Spirit.
(All pray silently for the gifts of the Holy Spirit.)

Ever loving God, may the Spirit you promised
fill us with your power and strength
that we may continue the work of Jesus here on earth.
We ask this through Jesus Christ, our Lord. Amen.

A psalm may also be prayed antiphonally by a group.

Begin by all singing the response: **Send forth your Spirit, O Lord,
and renew the face of the earth.**

Side one   Bless the Lord, my soul!
Lord God, how great you are.

Side two   How many are your works, O Lord!
The earth is full of your riches.
Response

Side one   You take back your Spirit, they die,
returning to the dust from which they came.

Side two   You send forth your Spirit, they are created;
and you renew the face of the earth.
Response

Side one   May the glory of God last for ever.
May God rejoice in all his works!

Side two   May my thoughts be pleasing to God.
I find my joy in the Lord.

Response

CELEBRATION BASED ON THE LITURGY OF THE WORD USING A GOSPEL READING _____

Theme: FRIENDSHIP

Preparation

Prepare the space and focal point.

The focal point will be the table of the Word with a place for the Book of the Word. For example:

- a cushion or a bookrest and a cover for the book, if needed
- a cloth for the table
- flowers
- candles *(if safe)*
- posters or artefacts related to the message of the text to be read
- pictures of friends who have helped each other and of people who have befriended others.

Decide on the number of readers and how the people and different groups mentioned in the Gospel will be represented. Jesus, centurion, servant, Jewish elders, crowd.

Gathering

Process the Book of the Word into the room and place it on the table of the Word.

Sing 'When I needed a neighbour were you there, were you there?' *(First verse only.)*

Greeting and Introduction.

Leader   *(A teacher, catechist or child(ren))* Welcomes those assembled and introduces the reading.

Today our reading is taken from the Gospel of St Luke and is the story of an extraordinary act of friendship between a Roman centurion and some Jewish people. A centurion was a Roman soldier in charge of a hundred men.

The Romans were an occupying army in Palestine in the time of Jesus and so not very popular with the local Jewish population.

The minister or ministers of the Word walk to the table of the Word and lift up the book. *(The reading is made from one book, not from pieces of paper unless previously placed inside the book.)*

Acclaim the Word

(Sing an alleluia verse)
Alleluia, alleluia, give praise to our risen Lord,
alleluia, alleluia, give praise to God's own Son.
(Repeat as necessary)

Proclaim the Word

R1　The Lord be with you.

All　And also with you.

R1　A reading from the holy Gospel according to Luke.

All　Glory to you Lord. *Sign forehead, lips and heart with a cross.*

R2　Jesus went into Capernaum, a town by the sea. There a centurion lived who had a servant who was sick and dying. Hearing about Jesus the centurion sent some Jewish leaders to find him and ask him to come and cure his servant.

R3　The Jewish leaders came to Jesus and pleaded earnestly with him.

R 4　The centurion deserves this favour of you because he is friendly towards our people. He has even built us a synagogue.

R2　So Jesus followed them to the centurion's house. He was not far from the house when some friends of the centurion met him with this message from the centurion:

R 5　Sir, do not inconvenience yourself by entering my house because I am not worthy to have you under my roof; it is for this reason that I did not come to ask a favour of you myself; but say the word and my servant will be healed.

R2　Jesus marvelled when he heard these words and turning to the crowd following him said:

R6　I have not found such great faith in Israel.

R5   And when the messengers returned to the house they found the servant restored to health.

R1   This is the Gospel of the Lord.

All   Praise to you, Lord Jesus Christ.

Conclude with a prayer.

CELEBRATION BASED ON THE PROFESSION OF FAITH

Preparation

Prepare the space and focal point.
In the focal point place the following:

- a Bible
- flowers
- candles (*if safe*)
- pictures of creation, Annunciation, Nativity, Risen Jesus (e.g Easter card), Pentecost, St Peter's, Pope, people of different nationalities, crucifix, statues or pictures of Our Lady and saints.

Gathering

Play peaceful music to gather the group.

Greeting and Introduction

Leader   *(Teacher, catechist or child)* We greet each other in the name of the Father and of the Son and of the Holy Spirit. Amen.

We gather together today to proclaim our Faith in God, Father, Son and Holy Spirit. The Faith of the Apostles whom Jesus called to spread God's kingdom on earth. With the Apostles let us say 'I believe' . . .

Everyone present repeats in turn 'I believe', *inserting their own name.* For example, 'I . . . Clare . . . believe.'

Group 1   We believe in God, the Father almighty, creator of heaven and earth.
(Place creation picture with focal point)

Group 2   We believe in Jesus Christ, his only Son, our Lord.
He was conceived by the power of the Holy Spirit –
(Place Annunciation scene with focal point)

Group 3   and born of the Virgin Mary.
(Place Nativity scene with focal point)

Group 4   He suffered under Pontius Pilate, was crucified, died and was buried. *(Place crucifix with focal point)*

Group 5   He descended to the dead. *(Moment of silence)*

Group 6   On the third day he rose again *(Play some joyful music and place Easter card with focal point)*

Group 7   He ascended into heaven, and is seated at the right hand of the Father.

Group 8   He will come again to judge the living and the dead.

Group 9   We believe in the Holy Spirit,
(Place Pentecost scene with focal point)
the holy catholic Church,
(Place picture of St Peter/Pope with focal point)
the communion of saints,
(Place pictures of all nationalities with focal point)
the forgiveness of sins,
the resurrection of the body,
and the life everlasting.
(Place pictures of Our Lady and the saints with focal point)

All   Amen.

Play peaceful music. Invite everyone to write their name on a card with the words 'I believe' and then to come forward and place their name card with the focal point.

CELEBRATION BASED ON THE PRAYER OF THE FAITHFUL _____

Preparation

Prepare the space and focal point.
In the focal point place:
- a Bible on a cushion or bookstand
- vase with some water in it
- flower for each person or group.

Gathering

Play the Taizé music 'O Lord hear my prayer' for a few moments to gather the group.

Greeting and Introduction

Leader *(Teacher, catechist or child)* We gather today . . . in the name of the Father and of the Son and of the Holy Spirit, to pray for the needs of our world.

Response *(Sung after each prayer)*
O Lord, hear my prayer, O Lord, hear my prayer,
when I call answer me.
O Lord, hear my prayer, O Lord, hear my prayer,
come and listen to me.

After each petition a flower is placed in the vase.

1. Let us pray for children suffering in countries at war . . .
   Lord give them your peace. *Sung response* O Lord, hear my prayer . . .

2. Let us pray for children who are sick . . .
   Lord give them your healing. *Sung response*

3. Let us pray for homeless children . . .
   Lord shelter them in your love. *Sung response*

Children continue with their own petitions.

Leader May God our loving and caring Father hear our prayers which we make through Jesus Christ our Lord. Amen.

Remember that the Prayers of the Faithful or General Intercessions are invitations to pray and are not in themselves prayers.

CELEBRATION BASED ON THE PREPARATION OF GIFTS

Theme

With a joyful heart we now prepare to give to God what God has first given to us.

This liturgy might be used on the completion of a task or piece of work or charity event.

Preparation

Prepare the space and focal point.
The focal point will be an empty table.

Gathering

Accompanied by the singing of a joyful song, a procession enters or processes around the room, bringing a cloth for the table, crucifix, Bible, (candles if safe), flowers.

'Give me joy in my heart, keep me praising.
Give me joy in my heart, I pray.
Give me joy in my heart, keep me praising.
Keep me praising now and everyday,' *etc.*

The table is then prepared.

Greeting and Introduction

Leader   *(A teacher, cathechist or child)* Welcomes those gathered and introduces the theme.
We gather today in the name of the Father and of the Son and of the Holy Spirit to praise and thank God for . . . *(for example)* the money we have raised for . . . completing our history project . . . good test results.

Procession of gifts

Accompany the procession of gifts by continuing the joyful song.

Gifts are given away not taken back, therefore use objects symbolising that for which the group is gathered to give thanks and praise. A large cheque could be made by the children to represent money donated. Test results can be a list of grades. A project can be a list of new knowledge gained, etc. Each child could bring something personally symbolic or something to give in charity.

Leader receives the gifts one by one and holds them up for all to see before placing them on the table.

All sing   Blest are you, Lord, God of all creation,
thanks to your goodness
these gifts we offer:
fruits of the earth, work of our hands
they will become our way to life.
Blessed be God! Blessed be God!
Blessed be God for ever! Amen!
(Repeat) Hymn 175, *Liturgical Hymns Old and New, Kevin Mayhew*

If many gifts are offered, sing between groups of gifts.

Prayer over the gifts

Leader   *(With arms extended)* Pray, my friends, that our sacrifice may be pleasing to God, our Almighty Father.

All   *(With heads bowed all pray silently)* May God receive our gifts for the praise and glory of his name, for our good, and for the good of all those in need.

Leader   Lord, may our gifts, offered in love, be pleasing to you and help us to follow Jesus with love.

All   AMEN.

CELEBRATION BASED ON THE PREFACE TO THE EUCHARISTIC PRAYER _____

Theme: ALL SAINTS

Preparation

Prepare the space and focal point.
In the focal point place:
* pictures of Our Lady, angels, saints.

Gathering

The introductory dialogue to the Eucharistic Prayer can be used to gather the group.

Leader	The Lord be with you.	*Extends arms, palms facing up, towards the group.*
Group	And also with you.	*Extend arms towards the leader.*
Leader	Lift up your hearts.	*Raises arms to shoulder level. Palms facing up.*
Group	We lift them up to the Lord.	*Raise arms.*
Leader	Let us give thanks to the Lord our God.	*Arms at waist level, palms facing up.*
Group	It is right to give God thanks and praise.	*Arms at waist level.*

Continue with the Preface.

Leader	Father all-powerful and ever-living God, we do well always and everywhere to give you thanks through Jesus Christ our Lord. We praise you for your gifts as we think today of all your saints in glory. We remember especially . . . *(children name the saints they want to include, for example St Anthony, patron of their school/church, etc.)* We remember Mary, mother of our Lord, who sang of the wonderful things you have done throughout the world *(children name some of the wonderful works of God).*

You raised Mary to be the mother of Jesus Christ, your Son, our Lord, the saviour of the world.

Through him the angels of heaven offer their prayer of adoration as they rejoice in your presence for ever.

With all the angels and saints in joy we sing to your glory . . .

All sing   *(Many musical accompaniments are available)*

Holy, holy, holy Lord,	*Arms raised to waist level.*
God of power and might,	*Arms raised to shoulder level.*
heaven and earth are full of your glory.	*Arms raised above head.*
Hosanna in the highest.	*Above head sway raised arms to left and right.*
Blessed is he who comes in the name of the Lord.	*Arms forward – waist level.*
Hosanna in the highest.	*Above head sway arms to left and right.*

Prayer

Leader   All holy God,
We praise your glory reflected in the saints.
May we, gathered here today,
like your saints be filled with love
and praise you with joy where Jesus is Lord for ever. Amen.

CELEBRATION BASED ON THE EUCHARISTIC PRAYER

When preparing children for first sacramental communion we practise them with an unconsecrated host and unconsecrated wine and the children realise that the bread and wine they are receiving is not Jesus because no priest has said the words of consecration over the bread and wine.

The object of this celebration based on the Eucharistic Prayer is to familiarise the children with the words and actions of what in reality takes place in the Mass.

Before this celebration takes place it is important to emphasise and make sure that the children understand that as there is no priest present there will be no consecration of the bread and wine. The bread and wine will not be changed into the body and blood of Christ at this celebration, it will be just bread and wine as there is no priest present to say the words of consecration. We do not have this power because we have not received the sacrament of Holy Orders which communicates the power of Christ, Our Lord to those who are ordained.

Several readers are involved in reading the prayers of this celebration.

An opportunity is provided here to explore the priestly vocation and the sacrament of Holy Orders. (Catechism of the Catholic Church, Part 2, Section 2, Chapter 3: Sacraments at the Service of Communion.)

This celebration is adapted from Eucharistic Prayer 1. Also introduce the children to Eucharistic Prayers 2, 3, 4 and the Eucharistic Prayers for children.

Preparation

Prepare the space and the focal point with:
- cloth
- candles (if safe)
- missal
- bread and wine.

Gathering

Sing a short song, for example, 'A new commandment' (135) or 'Bread is blessed and broken' (181), *Liturgical Hymns Old and New*, Kevin Mayhew; or any suitable hymn.

Greeting and Introduction

Leader   We gather today in the name of the Father and of the Son and of the Holy Spirit to remember how, on the night before he died,

Jesus gave us the bread of life and the saving cup and said, 'Do this in memory of me.'

Reader 1 When the hour came Jesus took his place at the table, and the apostles with him.
He said to them, 'I have longed to eat this passover with you before I suffer; because I will not eat it again until it is fulfilled in the kingdom of God.'

All We worship you, we give you thanks, we give you praise and glory.

Reader 2 The day before he suffered Jesus took bread in his sacred hands and looking up to heaven, to you his almighty Father, he gave you thanks and praise.
He broke the bread, gave it to his disciples, and said:
'Take this all of you and eat it:
This is my body which will be given up for you.'

All We worship you, we give you thanks, we give you praise and glory.

Reader 3 When supper was ended he took the cup.
Again he gave you thanks and praise.
He gave the cup to his disciples and said:
'Take this, all of you, and drink from it:
This is the cup of my blood,
the blood of the new and everlasting covenant.
It will be shed for you and for all
so that sins may be forgiven.
Do this in memory of me.'

All We worship you, we give you thanks, we give you praise and glory.

Conclude by singing hymn 219, 'Come on and celebrate' or 276, 'Give thanks with a grateful heart' or 616, 'Sing a new song unto the Lord' from *Liturgical Hymns Old and New* (Kevin Mayhew) or any suitable song of praise.

Share some festive food with the children after this celebration, not the bread and wine forming the display in the focal point.

CELEBRATION BASED ON THE INTERCESSIONS FOR THE CHURCH, THE DEAD, IN COMMUNION WITH THE SAINTS _____

Preparation

Prepare the space and the focal point:

- a table
- pictures representing the Church, saints
- pictures or names or symbols of the dead.

Gathering

Sing 'Through our lives and by our prayers your kingdom come' or 'O Lord, hear our prayer'.

Greeting and Introduction

Leader   Today we gather to remember and to pray for the Church throughout the world, for our relatives, our friends and for all who have died, and also for ourselves.
Let us begin our celebration in the name of the Father and of the Son and of the Holy Spirit. Amen.

Reader 1   Let us pray for the Church.
Lord, we remember those for whom the sacrifice of the Mass is offered . . . our Pope . . . our Bishop . . . our priests.

A picture of the Pope, the Bishop and names of the clergy to be prayed for are placed on the table.

All pray   Lord, remember us here present and all your people everywhere, and all people who seek you with a sincere heart.

Sing   Repeat the gathering refrain.

Reader 2   Let us pray for the dead.
We remember those who have died in the peace of Christ.

Pupils place on the table pictures or names of the deceased they want to pray for and speak the name the person aloud.

All pray Lord we pray for these and for all the dead whose faith is known to you alone.

Sing Repeat the gathering refrain.

Reader 3 Let us pray in communion with the saints.
Father, have mercy on us, your children
and make us worthy to enter heaven
in the company of Mary, the mother of God,
(Place picture of Mary on the table)
your apostles,
(Place picture of apostles on the table)
and all your saints.
(Place pictures of saints on the table)

All pray Father, may we praise you in union with them and give you glory
through your Son Jesus Christ.
Through him, with him, in him,
in the unity of the Holy Spirit,
all glory and honour is yours, almighty Father,
for ever and ever.
AMEN.

CELEBRATION BASED ON THE RITE OF DISMISSAL

An afternoon prayer at the end of the day or meeting.

Preparation

Prepare the space and focal point.

Gathering

A silent time of reflection to look over the day and to give thanks.

Leader   At the end of our day we bow our heads and pray for God's blessing.

Lord, grant us your love and protection this night and every night. Amen.

Lord, protect us and keep us safe from harm this night. Amen.

Lord, make us kind and loving like Jesus your Son. Amen.

Almighty God, Father, Son and Holy Spirit, bless us this night and always. Amen.

Let us go in peace to spread the joy of the Lord.

Children can be given opportunities to prepare the blessings for the close of the day.

CELEBRATING MASS

Mass to mark a new beginning.

Theme: FRIENDSHIP

Preparation

The atmosphere of the assembly and action of the community is affected by the way in which the space for worship is arranged. It is more dignified for children to be seated on chairs in preference to the floor.

Prepare a banner or altar frontal on which everyone in the group writes their name.

Gathering

Play suitable music as the children gather.

Introductory Rites

Entrance Song

The celebrant and ministers approach the altar (cross-bearer, acolytes, reader, ministers of communion and banner).

Celebrant's greeting

Introduction of the theme
(Teacher, catechist or child)
For example: Today we are gathered to celebrate a new beginning. It is a time when we renew old friendships and make new ones. A time to welcome new members of staff and new pupils (invite new members to stand).

Penitential Rite
Keep very brief or omit.

Gloria
See page 49. As this is a special occasion, include this great hymn of praise.

Opening Prayer
Remember the four elements of this prayer.

Have a marked moment of silence.

The community can hold their hands in the 'orans' position in imitation of the priest.

The priest prays the opening prayer which expresses the theme of the celebration.

Let us pray

In faith and love we ask you, Father, to watch over your family of *N* [name of school or church] gathered here.

As we grow in love of you may we grow in love of each other. We make our prayer . . .

Liturgy of the Word.

Only the Gospel reading must be included in Masses with children (*Directory of Children's Masses*).

The Gospel Procession and Acclamation

As the book of the Gospel is processed from the altar to the lectern accompanied by acolytes (with lighted candles if possible), all stand and sing the Alleluia.

Proclamation of the Word

See page 19.

Homily

Development of a point from the scripture of the day. See page 21.

Profession of Faith

Optional or a simplified form may be used or a dialogue; for example:

Do you believe in God the Father almighty, creator of heaven and earth?
We do.

Do you believe in Jesus Christ, God's only Son, our Lord who was conceived by the power of the Holy Spirit, born of the Virgin Mary, suffered under Pontius Pilate, was crucified, died and was buried? **We do.**

Do you believe that on the third day he rose again, he ascended into heaven, he is seated at the right hand of God, he will come again? **We do.**
Do you believe in the Holy Spirit, the holy catholic Church, the communion of saints, the forgiveness of sins, the resurrection of the body and life everlasting? **We do.**

General Intercessions

See page 22.

Liturgy of the Eucharist

Preparation of the altar
See page 24.

Procession with gifts and song
See page 24.

Preparation of the gifts
See *Masses for Children.*

Prayers over the gifts of bread and wine
Lord, accept the gifts we offer and may this Eucharist we share help us to grow in friendship and faith.

Eucharistic Prayer

Preface and Holy, holy
See *Masses for Children* and also pages 27 and 28.

Epiclesis

Consecration of the bread and wine.
It is permissible to ring a bell just before the consecration of the bread and the wine.

Intercessions for the Church
See page 30.

Memorial Acclamation
This should always be sung together with the **Great Amen.**

The Communion Rite

The Lord's Prayer
Preferably said.

Rite of Peace
Can be accompanied by music, not a hymn.

Lamb of God
This can take the form of a sung litany.

Communion Procession

Accompany this procession with a chant or refrain which does not require the use of hymn books. For example: 'Give me joy in my heart keep me praising . . .'

Silent Thanksgiving

Prayer after Communion

Lord, may the Eucharist we have shared help us to remain faithful to you and may it teach us the way to everlasting life. Amen.

Concluding Rite – Dismissal

Greeting

Blessing

It may be appropriate to have a special blessing for all new members of the community who can be invited forward at this point and who then leave the assembly in the recessional procession.

A hymn may be sung.

PLANNING EUCHARISTIC LITURGY _____

Introductory Rites

Welcome
Preparation and sending of invitations.
Reception of participant.
Other marks of hospitality.

Entrance Procession
Preceded by theme material – banners, art work, posters, dance, music.

Introduction of Theme
Spoken, mimed, sung, posters, dance.

Penitential Rite (Depending on season)
Spoken, sung, mimed, danced.

Gloria (Depending on season)
Sung, danced.

Opening Prayer
Printed out in large letters.

Liturgy of the Word

First Reading
Optional, may be children's written work.

Responsorial Psalm
Sung, recited antiphonally, danced.

Gospel Acclamation
Procession of book of the Gospels.
Music, percussion, dance, lights, incense.

Proclamation of the Gospel
Read, sung, illustrated, several readers.

Homily
Dialogue, given by adult other than priest, mimed.

Profession of Faith
Said, sung, dialogue, illustrated.

General Intercessions
Individual voices, sung responses, illustrated.

Liturgy of the Eucharist
Preparation
Setting of table.

Procession of gifts (Bread and Wine) and song
Hymn, music, dance, silence.

Preparation of the gifts
Sung with actions.

Eucharistic Prayer
Introductory dialogue
Said, sung with raising of arms.

Preface
Illustrated.

Holy, holy
Sung, danced, percussion.

Memorial Acclamation
Sung, percussion, gesture.

Prayer for the Church
Litany, illustrations, individual names.

Great Amen
Sung.

Communion Rite

Lord's Prayer
Said.

Rite of Peace
Gesture.

Breaking of Bread
Lamb of God . . . Litany. Sung. Compose own words.

Communion Procession
Accompany with singing.

Song of Praise and Thanksgiving
Read reflection, prayer, dance, hymn.

Concluding Rites

Blessing, dismissal, recessional procession
Music, song, silence.

It is not necessary to sing hymns all the way through the Mass. The suggestions given here are not for entertainment but to help focus the children on the part of the Mass being celebrated and to bring out the meaning of what is being done.

Just as we do not want to overload the Mass with hymns, neither do we want to overload it with drama, dance or anything else.

The aim is to enable the children to participate more fully in the Mass with a deeper and fuller understanding of what is being done and why, and to enable them to enter prayerfully into the action of the Mass. To bring them to that moment when they hear Jesus calling them and feel him laying his hand upon them in blessing.

REFERENCES AND RELATED READING

Sacrosanctum Concilium, Documents of Vatican II, 1963.

Directory of Children's Masses, Catholic Truth Society, 1973.

Catechism of the Catholic Church, Geoffrey Chapman, 1994.

Liturgy of the Word with Children – Guidelines, Bishops' Conference of England and Wales, 1996, Liturgy Office, 39 Eccleston Square, London.

The Word and Eucharist Handbook, Lawrence J. Johnson, Resource Publication Inc, 1986.

Spirit and Song of the New Liturgy, Lucien Deiss C.S.Sp. World Library Publications Inc, 1976.

How to Understand the Liturgy, Jean Lebon, SCM Press Ltd, 1986.

Liturgical Hymns Old and New, Kevin Mayhew, 1999.

Rejoice! Rejoice!, Cathy Lee, Dove Communications, 1983.